Dedicated to the Music Ministry of
st United Methodist Church, Kerrville, Texas
Rev. Don McAvoy, Jr., Minister of Music

WHISPERS
of the
PASSION

by Joseph M. Martin

Orchestration by Brant Adams

CONTENTS

Performance Time: Approximately 35 minutes

① This symbol indicates a track number on
the StudioTrax CD (Accompaniment Only).

Harold Flammer
MUSIC

A DIVISION OF SHAWNEE PRESS, INC.
EXCLUSIVELY DISTRIBUTED BY HAL LEONARD CORPORATION

Visit Shawnee Press Online at
www.shawneepress.com

Foreword

As Lenten shadows fall, we silence ourselves to listen for that still small voice whispering in the night.

With hopeful ears, we strain to discover some calming assurance, some comforting word. Our empty dreams reach out for healing and solace. In the quiet chapels of the heart, we pause and listen, waiting for an answer.

As we think of the cross, the crown of thorns, the scarlet robe, the chalice, and the palms, we hear their silent witness. Across the ages, their stories sing to us, and we are compelled to listen. In hushed tones, they remind us of the cost of redemption and of the Savior's matchless love. Through their testimony, we find our way to the place of healing and illumination.

In the stillness of these sacred moments, pause in silent wonder at the miracle of mercy and surround your spirit with the deep abundance of God's love. Come to the silence and solitude of the shadows and listen for the whispers of the passion. Lay aside the clamor of the world, and for a season, lose yourself in the music of grace.

JOSEPH M. MARTIN

Performance Notes

"Whispers of the Passion" is a cantata offering the option of 5 spoken soliloquies that can be presented between each of the choral numbers. These brief monologues feature the "voices" of the "silent witnesses" to Christ's passion. The voices include: the Ancient Walls of Jerusalem, the Chalice, the Robe, the Crown of Thorns, and the Cross. These monologues are followed by a choral response that relates to the "lesson and message" presented by each of these witnesses.

To help the congregants connect with this unusual perspective, you may want to use the "Digital Resource Kit" that contains support material intended to accompany this work. Images appropriate to each soliloquy can be displayed during the narrative to clarify and amplify the power of the reading. To further enhance each soliloquy, another option would be to bring forward a representation of the appropriate character to place on the altar or at the front of the auditorium.

     Palms in a vase or a weathered stone
     A chalice for Communion
     A purple cloth representing the robe
     A crown of thorns
     A cross

These can be arranged progressively upon the altar or on a table as the work is presented to create a visual collage for the presentation.

Banners may also be used to help deliver the message of this work.

An extended introduction is provided on "Contemplation of the Cross" should a procession of the cross be desired or extra time be needed for arranging all of the featured elements upon the altar for this final number. The cross can be placed in the center with the purple cloth wrapped around the base. Palms can be arranged at the base of the cross or placed on the edges of the table in a vase. The crown of thorns can be cradled at the top of the cross in the traditional manner. The chalice can also be placed at the base of the cross or to the side of the altar.

These extra visual elements are all optional and intended to energize the director's own creativity when presenting the cantata.

WHISPERS OF THE PASSION
Prologue

Music by
JOSEPH M. MARTIN (BMI

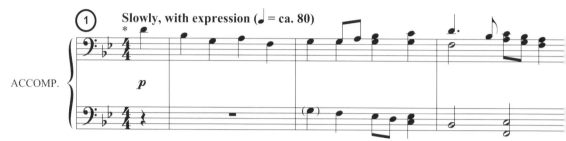

* Tune: SALVATION, *Kentucky Harmony*, 1816

A SOLEMN INVITATION

Words and music by
JOSEPH M. MARTIN (BMI)

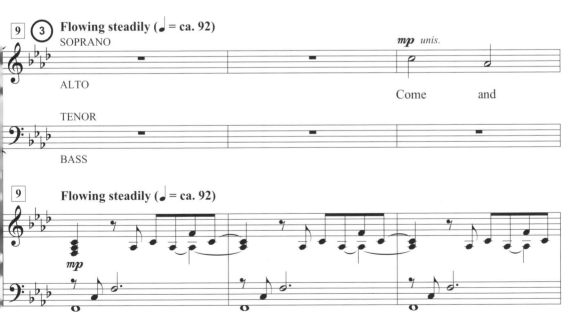

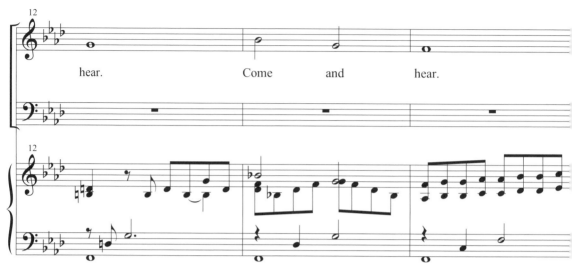

hear. Come and hear.

Find words of hope and let your spir - it be re -

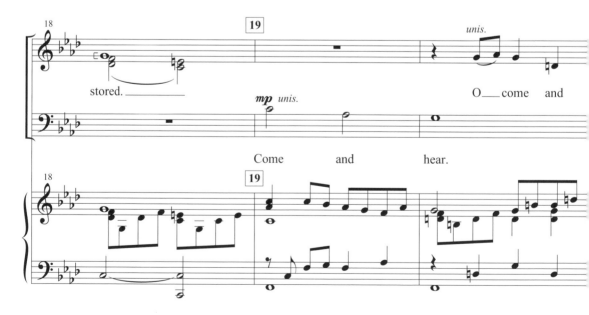

stored. O come and

mp unis.

Come and hear.

8

9

lay a-side. Lis-ten to the words of life.

Come, in re-mem-brance of the Lord.

Come and re-mem-ber the Lord.

The Walls and Gates of Jerusalem

I am the ancient walls and gates of Jerusalem.

I have stood sentinel through the ages to this great city of might. I have seen the tragedy and sorrow of lost conflicts and heard the shouts of victory and triumph. I have been witness to the stoning of prophets and the crowning of kings. Long I have waited for the day when heaven would send a deliverer to set the people free from their oppression and inspire the hearts and souls of the nation.

Today I hear hosannas and cries of joy from the people. I see a procession that is different from others that have come before. The palm branches are waving high, signaling the arrival of a military hero, but this is no king crowned from violence. This is the Prince of Peace, whose government will rest on shoulders of justice and truth.

This is the one of whom Isaiah wrote, "Lift up your heads, ye mighty gates; and be lifted up ye everlasting doors, and let the King of glory come in."

Yes, I can hear it in the whisper of the palms and the shouts of the multitudes. The Lord of Hosts has come to comfort and redeem His people. Blessed is He who comes in the name of the Lord!

WHISPER OF THE PALMS

Words and music by
JOSEPH M. MARTIN (BMI)

Je - sus rides on by the tow - ers of Zi - on.

Joy - ful ho - san - nas re - sound through the air.

Slow - ly He rides through the streets of the cit - y.

Is this the one that the proph - ets de - clared?

Lis-ten to the whis-per of the palms.

Ooo

Ooo

unis.

rit.

Joy - ful ho - san - nas will turn in - to jeers.

Wave the palms slow - ly. Lay the palms gen - tly.

Hon - or the King with a ju - bi - lant psalm. Wave the palms slow - ly.

Lay the palms gen - tly. Bring forth the branch - es of wor - ship and praise.

Lis - ten to the whis - per of the palms.

Je - sus still moves through our tem - ples and church - es.

Prais - es still ring from our tow - ers of stone. The

worship we offer is rich with ho-san-nas, yet

Je-sus still car-ries the cross__ a-lone._____

Wave the palms slow-ly. Lay the palms bold-ly.

The Chalice

I am the chalice, the grail of mercy.

I hold the wine for the Passover Feast. I help the faithful celebrate their most sacred occasions. I am the cup of redemption lifted high to celebrate the passing over of death and pestilence during the captivity in Egypt.

Tonight I am prepared for this important feast. With careful ritual, I am placed on the table next to loaves of unleavened bread and bitter herbs ready for my role as the vessel of grace.

As I receive the wine, I realize there is something different about this night. The Rabbi who holds me now is praying ancient prayers, but teaching of new covenants. His words fill the room with hope and with wonder.

Then suddenly there is a turning as dark shadows fall across the upper room. The Rabbi speaks now of betrayal and death. He searches the eyes of those gathered around the table. Suddenly, one of the men steals away into the night fleeing His gaze.

As the man's footsteps fade into the darkness, hope seems to return to the room. With a gentle hand this one they call Jesus blesses the wine, lifts me to his lips, and changes the world.

NOCTURNE OF GRACE

Tune: **SALVATION**
Kentucky Harmony, 1816
Arranged by
JOSEPH M. MARTIN(BMI)

night that Je - sus was be - trayed, a sa - cred meal _ was

Pas - chal __ meal, to share the __ gift __ of grace.

They gath - ered close to

Flowing, with energy (♩. = 112-116)

Je - sus as night grew dark and deep.

As shad - ows fell a - cross the room, their

Ah, _____ hearts be - gan to weep. Then

hearts be - gan to weep. _____

Ju - das quick - ly left them all and ran in - to the

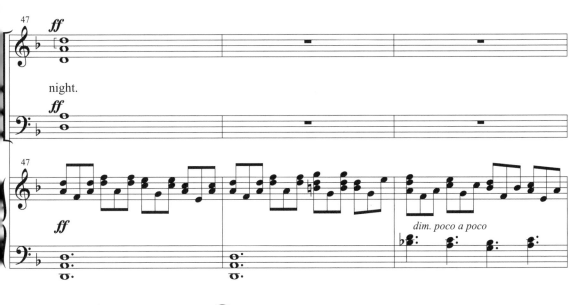

night.

Be -

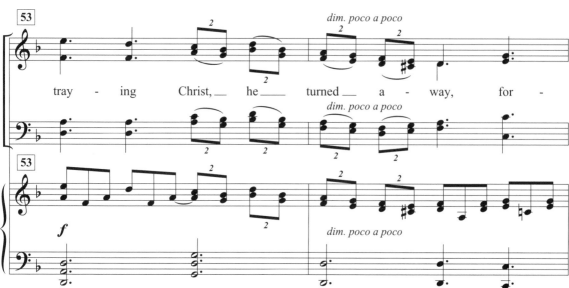

tray - ing Christ, __ he __ turned __ a - way, for -

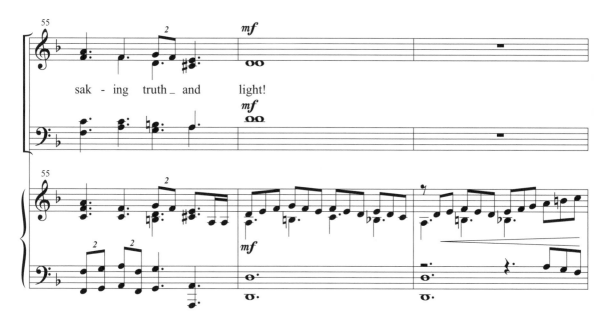

sak - ing truth __ and light!

He took the cup of sor - row and

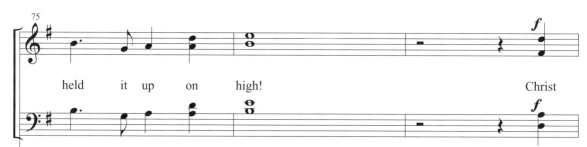

held it up on high! Christ

blessed the wine of mer - cy. He broke the bread of

life. God's cov - e - nant_ of_ grace_ was made and

sealed in love that night.

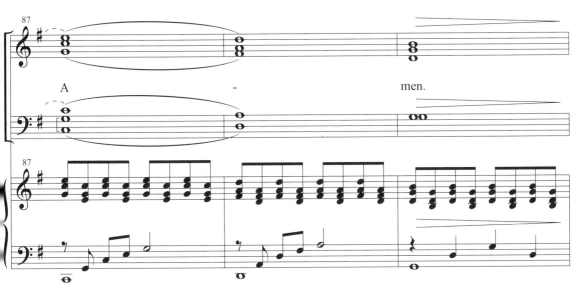

A - men.

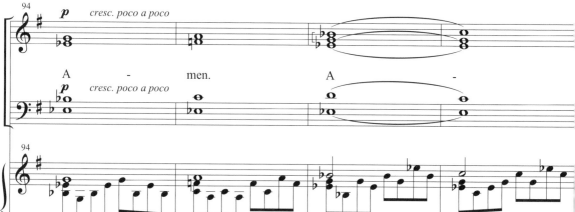

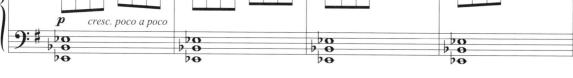

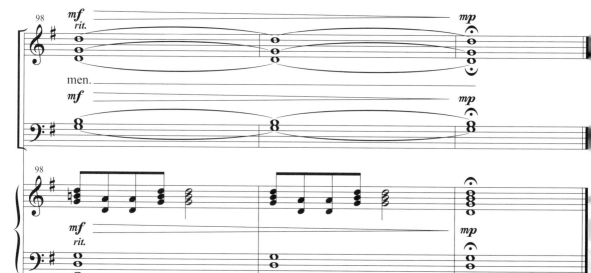

The Robe

I am the robe, the vestment of shame.

I was once a beautiful garment of the highest quality. Woven from the finest purple, I was destined to adorn the back of a governor or king. At the most solemn ceremonies, I would have been called into service. At the sight of my royal colors, there would be pageantry and pomp. At the festive sound of the trumpet, they would have announced my owner, and the court would have bowed in reverence as we entered the room.

All that has changed. Now I am an obscenity - the object of ridicule and scorn. My silken threads are ruined; stained with the tears and sweat of a condemned man. My splendor is made into a cruel joke as they drape me around His wounded body. They have beaten Him with whips, and His wounds are pouring out a crimson stream of misery.

Soon the cruel Centurions will cast lots for me… like some souvenir of sorrow. Nothing can remove the stain I bear; so deep it has penetrated my very being.

I am repulsive and ugly. I am beyond redemption… for I am covered by the blood of this one they call Jesus.

commissioned by the Chancel and Youth Choirs of First United Methodist Church, Gainesville, Georgia,
in Celebration and Honor of Sam Marley's 30 years of service to Youth, Music and Missions

REDEEMER OF MY HEART

Words by
J. PAUL WILLIAMS (ASCAP), *alt.*
Based on *Psalm 139*

Music by
JOSEPH M. MARTIN (BMI)

When I rise to greet the morn-ing, Lord, I find You there.

When I call in the night, You are with me. Lord, You hear my prayer.

30
a tempo
p
When I turn my heart from heav - en,
p
30
a tempo
p
33
mp
when I fall and go a - stray,
mp
33
mp
36
mf
cresc. poco a poco
like a shep - herd, Lord, You find me.
mf
cresc. poco a poco
36
mf
cresc. poco a poco

42

Search me, Lord, and know me, Re-deem-er of my heart. Search me. Know me. Re-veal my in-most part._____ Cov-er me with

Shine Your love on me, O___ Lord,___ Re-deem-er of my

heart. Search me, Lord, and know me, Re -

deem - er of my heart.___

The Crown of Thorns

I am the crown of thorns, the twisted vines of affliction.

I once was a proud protector of the precious rose. I defended the blossom from injury; piercing all those who would do it harm. I was strong and was feared by all who entered the garden. I served with faithfulness the most exquisite flowers of spring. Those who saw my master were filled with hope and wonder.

Now, I am a tool of torture. Misshapen and wraped into a crown, I am pressed into the flesh of a man who is being executed. Forced into place, I engrave my image into His brow and His blood pours out at my cruel touch. Who is this One who is treated with such violence? What crime could He have been guilty of?

How I long to touch my beloved rose again. My heart aches to know its graceful fragrance and to be a part of the vine that brought such beauty to the world. I am lost without the rose. If only I could find my way back to the garden.

*In honor of Johnny Matlock and Alexis Robinson for their dedication to the music ministry
by the First United Methodist Church Chancel Choir, Hays, Kansas*

O LOVE THAT WILL NOT LET ME GO

Words by
GEORGE MATHESON (1842-1906)

Music by
JOSEPH M. MARTIN (BMI)

48

I yield my flick-'ring torch to Thee.

My heart re-stores its bor-rowed ray, that in the sun-shine's

blaze its day may bright-er, fair-er be.

O Love that will not let me go,

O Love that will not let me go.

O Joy that seeks me through my

pain, _____ I can - not close my heart to

Thee. _____ I trace the rain - bow through the

rain, and know the prom - ise is not vain, morn will tear - less

54

depths its flow may rich - er, full - er be._____

O love that will not let me go,

O love that will not let me go,_____

The Cross

I am the cross, the weeping tree.

I was once a mighty tree bursting with life, planted beside peaceful waters. People rested in my shade and children played upon my limbs. I was a blessing to the traveler and a home for singing birds. I brought forth fruit and whispered quietly when the wind moved through my branches in praise to my Creator.

Then I was cut down in my prime and fashioned into an instrument of death. Like the man who hangs in my embrace, I was stripped of my dignity. I stand twisted and dying, a loathsome object that all turn away from. My arms grow weary with the pitiful fruit I am forced to hold. The iron nails have splintered my spirit, and the moans of a dying man have replaced the calls of the nightingale. I am dying and soon I will be forgotten. If only I had been able to meet a carpenter who could have made me into something beautiful… something that could have honored my Creator. Who will ever remember a rugged cross?

CONTEMPLATION OF THE CROSS

Words by
JOSEPH M. MARTIN

Based on tunes
HAMBUR
by LOWELL MASON (1792-187...
EVENTID
by WILLIAM HENRY MONK (1823-188...
Arranged by
JOSEPH M. MARTIN (BM...

ACCOMP.

* Tune: HAMBURG, Lowell Mason, 1792-1872

Come to the cross. Be-

hold the Lamb of grace. Kneel ___ in the shad - ows.

Find your hid - ing place._____ Hum - ble your -

self up - on the crim - son sod._____

Come____ to the cross and know the heart of____

God.

Mine is the sin, but Thine the right - teous - ness.

See, from His head, His____ hands His____

WHISPERS OF THE PASSION - SATB

62

WHISPERS OF THE PASSION - SATB

robe, my ref - uge, and my peace,

Thy blood, Thy righ - teous - ness, O Lord, my

God.

Did e'er such love and _____ sor - row _____

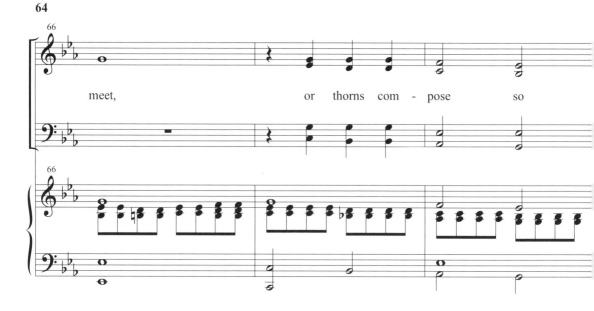

meet,   or thorns com - pose   so

rich   a___   crown.

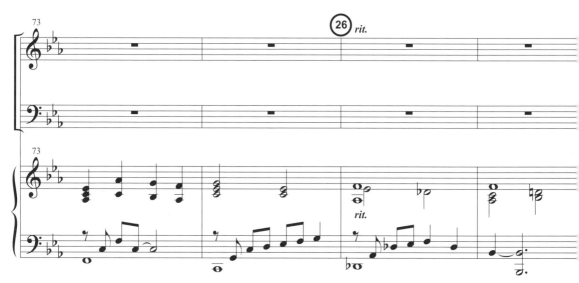

Hold Thou Thy cross before my long - ing eyes. Shine through the gloom and point me to the skies. *A - maz - ing love! how can it be that Thou my God should die for me, that Thou my God should die for

*Words: Charles Wesley, 1707-1788

WHISPERS OF THE PASSION - SATB

66